THE BATTLE AGAINST
BOREDOM

THE ADVENTURES OF THE HORNED AVENGER & BLT

Adventure #1 - How to Draw Cartoons

THE HORNED AVENGER™

Ben Adams   **Ray Nelson**   **Doug Kelly**

THE HORNED AVENGER™

Story:
Ray Nelson
Ben Adams

Art Direction:
Ben Adams

Pencils & Inking:
Ben Adams
Ray Nelson
Douglas Kelly

Animal Trainer:
Mike McLane

Costumes:
Chris Nelson
Holly McLane

Computer:
Ben Adams
Ray Nelson
Julie Hansen
Kyle Holveck
Aaron Peeples
Kari Rasmussen
Matt Adams
Brud Giles

Editing:
Brian Feltovich

SOMETIME IN THE FUTURE •••

Email The Horned Avenger at:
avenger@flyingrhino.com

Flying Rhinoceros
P.O. Box 3989 Portland, Oregon 97208
www.flyingrhino.com

ISBN 1-59168-010-7
Library of Congress Control Number: 2002100269

OUT OF THE RUBBLE CLIMBS THE HORNED AVENGER, THE ONLY HOPE FOR PLANET EARTH. A HULKING FIGURE, HE PULLS HIMSELF TO THE TOP OF THE WRECKAGE TO SURVEY THE SCENE BELOW. HIS MUSCLES RIPPLE AS HE SWINGS HIS MAMMOTH HEAD FROM LEFT TO RIGHT. WHAT WAS ONCE A LAUGHING PLANET IS NOW THE PLAYGROUND OF BOREDOM . . . BARON VON BOREDOM!!!!

HEY, MUSCLE BOY! DO YOU THINK YOU COULD QUIT FLEXING FOR JUST A SECOND AND HELP ME UP?

SORRY, BLT.

AN UNLIKELY PAIR INDEED, THE HORNED AVENGER AND BLT PREPARE TO FULFILL THEIR DESTINY. THE FATE OF EVERY BEING ON THIS ONCE THRIVING PLANET NOW RESTS IN THE HOOVES OF OUR HEROES.

IT ALL BEGAN . . . WHEN A SMALL BOY NAMED ELMER WAINWRIGHT TURNED IN AN ART PROJECT. ELMER WAS QUITE PROUD OF THIS PROJECT. HE HAD DRAWN A DETAILED SCENE OF ALIEN SPACE MONSTERS EATING THE HEADS OFF A CROWD OF FRIGHTENED TOWNSPEOPLE. (ELMER'S DRAWING WAS KIND OF GROSS, BUT IT WAS A REALLY CREATIVE PIECE OF WORK.) WHEN ELMER TURNED IN HIS MASTERPIECE, HE RECEIVED A HARSH LECTURE FROM HIS TEACHER. HE WAS TOLD THAT GRASS IS ALWAYS GREEN AND SKIES ARE ALWAYS BLUE. THE TEACHER ALSO SAID THAT ALIENS EATING TOWNSPEOPLE WASN'T AN APPROPRIATE TOPIC FOR ART AND THAT WE SHOULD ALWAYS COLOR INSIDE THE LINES.

THIS CRUSHED POOR ELMER. EVERY OUNCE OF CREATIVITY WAS SUCKED FROM THE LITTLE BOY. THEN ONE DAY, AFTER WATCHING A TWELVE-HOUR "BRADY BUNCH" MARATHON, LITTLE ELMER WAINWRIGHT STOOD UP AND YELLED . . .

I'M NOT GOING TO TAKE IT ANYMORE!

"FROM THIS DAY FORWARD, I WILL BE KNOWN AS **BARON VON BOREDOM** AND THE REST OF THE WORLD WILL SUFFER ALONG WITH ME. IF I CANNOT BE CREATIVE, I WILL DRAG EVERY OTHER LIVING CREATURE INTO THE DEPTHS OF BOREDOM WITH ME. THIS PLANET WILL NEVER AGAIN SEE GRASS THAT IS GREEN OR SKIES THAT ARE BLUE!"

CARTOONING IS ALL ABOUT TAKING CHANCES AND TRYING NEW STUFF. DON'T WORRY ABOUT MAKING EVERY DRAWING PERFECT. DON'T SPEND MOST OF YOUR TIME ERASING. IF YOU THINK YOU'VE MESSED UP, KEEP GOING. YOU NEVER KNOW, YOU MIGHT END UP WITH THE BEST DRAWING YOU'VE EVER DONE.

ALL RIGHT, H.A.! I GET IT! WHERE DO I START?

TOOLS

The first step is to pick the tools that you want to use. All you need is something to draw with and something to draw on. Don't be afraid to experiment with new and unusual tools.

Sketchpad

The sketchpad is one of the most important tools you will work with. You can purchase a sketchpad at any art or variety store. They can cost as little as $2 or as much as $30. If you can't get to the store or don't have any money, gather some old scrap paper and staple it together. Do all of your experimenting and rough drawings in the sketchpad. It's like a storage space for your ideas.

Pens

There are many different styles of pens. Use your sketchbook to try them all. When you test a pen in your sketchbook, write down what kind it is next to the drawing. That way, if you like the style you can use it again. Even simple ballpoint pens can make a great cartoon. Remember: the same pen on different types of paper may look completely different.

Pencils

Pencils come in different shapes, colors, and sizes. Experiment. Try using pencils that are sharp and pencils that are dull. Try using the point and then the side of the lead.

Brushes

If you use ink or paint, you'll need some brushes. Brushes can be very fine for detail work or very thick for coloring large spaces. Always clean your brushes when you're done so they don't get ruined!

Crayons

The Horned Avenger always carries a bunch of color crayons. (It doesn't matter how old you are, crayons are great for cartooning.) Crayons allow you to add a quick burst of color to your cartoons. For a great effect, try coloring with crayons and then painting over your cartoon with watercolor paints.

Chalk

Colored chalk can give you some really cool effects. Try chalk on rough paper, a chalkboard, or on the sidewalks around your home.

Paints

Like the other tools, paints come in all different colors and types. Watercolors and acrylics are great to use because of their bright colors. They are also easier to clean up than oil paints.

Photocopier

A photocopier is a gold mine for a cartoonist. Your teacher or parents might be able to make copies for you. There are also stores that specialize in making copies. Take one of your really awesome cartoons and make a bunch of copies. This will allow you to experiment with different colors. Another neat trick is to slowly pull the cartoon as it is being copied. This will distort your drawing, giving you some strange results. All of this is fun and doesn't ruin the original drawing.

Cardboard

Try drawing your cartoons on cardboard. You can cut them out, and they will stand up by themselves.

Paper

You might not know it, but there are thousands of types of paper. Some paper is smooth and some is bumpy. Some paper is waterproof and some really soaks up paint and ink. Try different types of paper with various pens, paints, and pencils.

Napkins

At some time or another, you'll have to wait for your food in the cafeteria or a restaurant. Next time this happens, grab a bunch of napkins and start drawing. Ballpoint pen ink on a napkin looks great.

Old Magazines

Grab a bunch of old magazines. Then pretend you're Dr. Frankenstein and cut out body parts. Glue the different body parts together to create wacky new cartoon characters.

Old Yearbooks

Ask parents or friends to dig up all of their old yearbooks. Yearbooks are the best places to find really weird names for your characters. You'll also get good ideas for cartoon faces and hairstyles.

Mixing Stuff

Try mixing all of your cartooning tools. Paint a background and glue a magazine monster character to it. Try drawing crayon characters and painting a watercolor background over it.

Modeling Clay

Clay offers a whole different world for cartooning. Take clay and build characters that you have drawn. Sometimes it is more difficult to build a character out of clay than it is to draw one because you have to decide what the character looks like from the side, back, and front!

STONE AGE CAVE PEOPLE USED TO DRAW ON CAVE WALLS WITH BARK AND BERRIES.

LET'S GET STARTED, SHALL WE?

LET'S GIVE HIM THE STANDARD HUMAN FACE, H.A.!

BLT! HAVE YOU FORGOTTEN THE ONLY RULE TO CARTOONING? THE ONLY RULE TO CARTOONING IS . . . **THERE ARE NO RULES!**

NO MATTER HOW HARD YOU TRY, YOU CAN'T DRAW A CARTOON WRONG. IF YOU WANTED TO GIVE THIS STICK FIGURE TWENTY-SEVEN EYEBALLS AND GREEN HAIR, YOU COULD. IF YOU WANTED TO GIVE HIM A COW'S HEAD AND THE BODY OF A HAMSTER, YOU COULD. THERE ARE NO RULES WHEN YOU ARE CARTOONING! DON'T WORRY ABOUT MESSING UP. SOME OF MY BEST CARTOONS WERE DRAWINGS THAT I THOUGHT I HAD MESSED UP. INSTEAD OF STARTING OVER, I KEPT DRAWING AND ENDED UP WITH SOMETHING NEW, COOL, AND UNEXPECTED!

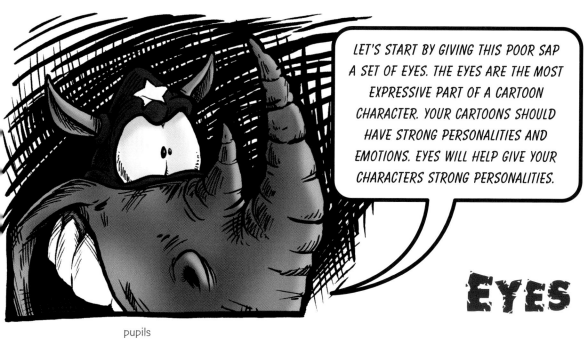

LET'S START BY GIVING THIS POOR SAP A SET OF EYES. THE EYES ARE THE MOST EXPRESSIVE PART OF A CARTOON CHARACTER. YOUR CARTOONS SHOULD HAVE STRONG PERSONALITIES AND EMOTIONS. EYES WILL HELP GIVE YOUR CHARACTERS STRONG PERSONALITIES.

EYES

pupils

dots

circles

teardrops

baggy eyes

droopy eyelids

big bucks

crazy eyes

YOU KNOW WHAT I LIKE TO DO? I LIKE TO MAKE THE PUPILS DIFFERENT SHAPES. I DRAW DOLLAR SIGNS WHEN A CHARACTER HAS FOUND LOTS OF MONEY. I DRAW THE PUPILS IN THE SHAPE OF LITTLE HEARTS WHEN THE CHARACTER IS IN LOVE. SOMETIMES I JUST MOVE THE PUPILS AROUND OR MAKE THEM DIFFERENT SIZES.

evil eyes

cute eyes

worried

angry

surprised

accusing

blank stare

tired

11

NOSES

The nose is the easiest feature to draw on a face. Start with a basic shape, such as a circle or a triangle. Don't be afraid to adjust the size and proportion of the nose shape.

REMEMBER, MY LITTLE FRIEND: YOU CAN PICK YOUR FRIENDS, AND YOU CAN PICK YOUR NOSE, BUT YOU CAN'T PICK YOUR FRIEND'S NOSE. HEH HEH!

Use a circle for a nose.

Draw a C for a nose.

Try a clover-leaf shape.

Use two sides of a triangle for a pointed nose.

Try stretching the nose down.

See how big you can make the nose.

Try turning the nose up and coloring in the nostril.

A bumpy pickle makes a weird nose. Add warts and hair for extra fun!

You can also add nostrils to a nose.

SNIFF! SNIFF! SNIFF!

When using shapes, such as a circle or a C, don't get stuck using only one version of that shape. Try stretching or squashing the shape for different looks.

normal

squashed

stretched

small

big

12

MOUTHS

One of the best ways to make a cartoon mouth is to draw a line. Try different types of lines—long, short, straight, crooked, squiggled, and jagged. After you get good at making line mouths, try a few open mouths. Don't forget to draw the teeth and tongue.

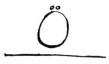

Here's a simple-line mouth.

Raise the line under the nose.

Use a jagged line.

Make a short-line mouth.

Use a slanted-line mouth.

Wrap the mouth all the way around the nose.

Try squiggling the line.

Try using a triangle, then add a tongue.

Try squishing the triangle.

Add a tongue and some teeth to an open mouth.

Not all teeth are perfect. Try different sizes and shapes.

Droop a tongue from the line. Add some slobber.

Draw a mouth from the side.

13

Horned Avenger Hint

What characters say or think tells us a lot about their personalities. Are they mean or nice? Serious or funny? Are they self-confident or do they get jealous easily? Dialogue can show us key elements of the plot or get the reader to laugh at a funny joke. When you draw your characters, what types of things are they going to say or think?

BODY SHAPES

When you first build cartoon characters, use simple shapes for their bodies.

circles and ovals

triangles

squares and rectangles

stretch shapes

MALE

Different body shapes and sizes create different personalities. Remember to exaggerate!

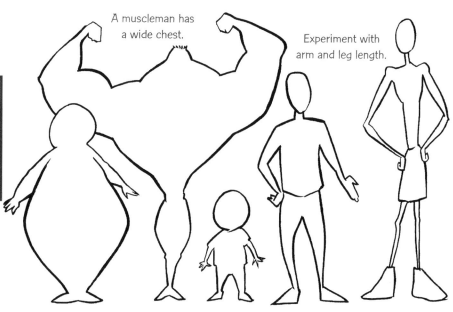

A muscleman has a wide chest.

Experiment with arm and leg length.

Expand the tummy for a cartoon couch potato.

Kids have big heads and little bodies.

A basketball player has a stretched-out body.

FEMALE

Cartoon women look different than male cartoons. Exaggerate different features to create even more characters.

Exaggerate the pinched waist to create a cartoon supermodel.

Use a triangle for a little girl's dress.

Try a bigger, rounder figure.

Horned Avenger Hint

Try moving a character's belt line for a new look.

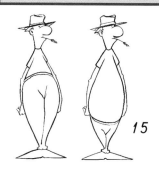

15

HEAD SHAPES

The head shape for a cartoon character doesn't always have to be round like a real human head. Think of a cartoon head as a big water balloon. When you squish the top, the bottom gets bigger. When you squeeze the bottom, the top gets bigger. Any shape can make a great cartoon head. In pencil, lightly sketch the shape you are going to use. You can then use the shape as a guide to build the head.

circle

square

oval stretched tall

triangle pointing up

triangle pointing down

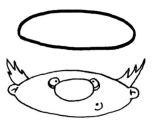

oval squished flat

Horned Avenger Hint

Ears can be made with a C shape and a backward C shape. Ears can be placed up high on a head or really low on a head. Try all kinds of different locations for the ears.

COMPOUND HEAD SHAPES

A compound shape is two shapes put together. Mix different head shapes to create a new cartoon character.

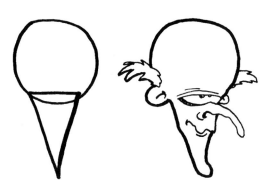

Place a circle on top of a triangle for an ice cream cone shape.

Add a rectangle to the top of a circle.

Try a triangle on top of a square.

Have the upper lip stick out for an overbite.

Have the lower lip stick out for an underbite.

PLACING FEATURES

Try creating different faces with the same head shape. Draw several circles the same size, and then move the features around the face. Also, experiment with different-sized features for a new look.

top

bottom

high and low

stretched across

large

small

To make a character successful, you need to add details. One of the best details you can add to a character is hair. Using a different hairstyle changes not only the look of a character but also its personality. Be inventive with the hairstyles you use. For reference, look through old magazines or yearbooks for different hairstyles.

MARCIA, MARCIA, MARCIA

MILITARY

PUNK PORKER

SANTA PORK

THE KING

DOLLY PORKER

ROCKER

MALL HAIR

MAD SCIENTIST

HAIR CLUB FOR PIGS

HANDLEBAR PIG *19*

EXPRESSIONS

YOU ARE ONE GOOD-LOOKIN' RHINO!

The best way to learn how to draw expressions is to look in a mirror. Study what every part of your face does when you make an expression. Look at your features and then try to draw that expression in your sketchpad. With practice, you'll be able to draw all kinds of expressions without even thinking about it.

GRRRRRR!

HAPPY, HAPPY, JOY, JOY!

YOU GOTTA BE KIDDIN' M

IT FIGURES!

CHEEEESE!

BOO-BOO LIP

HUBBA, HUBBA!

THIS CAN'T BE HAPPENING!

BRAIN CRAMP

OUCH! OUCH! OOOOO!

WORRIED

NOT IMPRESSED

HEH HEH HEH!

AUGHHH!

WHAT ARE YOU LOOKIN' AT?!

WAHHHHH!

OOOOOPS!

ZZZZZZZ

BONK!

DID I DO THAT?

Horned Avenger Hint

Don't underestimate the importance of giving your characters extreme expressions. People love characters with personality. Expressions help give your characters personality.

21

EXTREME EXPRESSIONS

WHEN DRAWING YOUR CHARACTERS, DON'T BE AFRAID TO MAKE THEIR EXPRESSIONS **REALLY** WILD. PEOPLE LOVE IT WHEN EYES BUG OUT AND JAWS DROP TO THE GROUND.

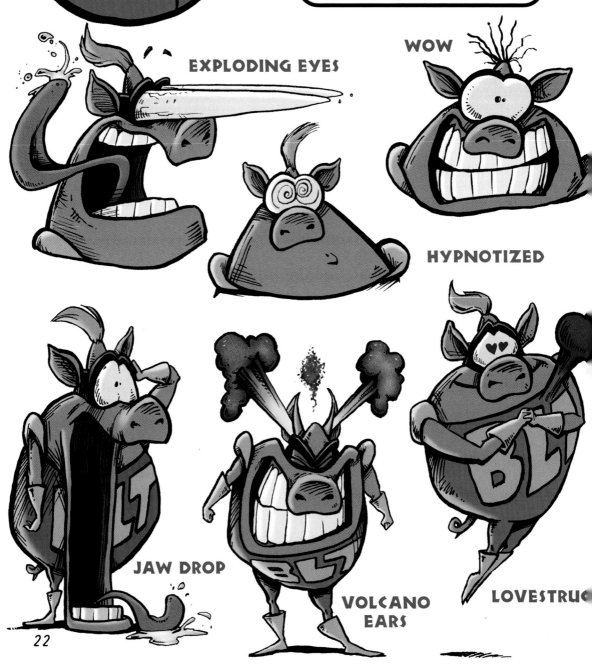

EXPLODING EYES

WOW

HYPNOTIZED

JAW DROP

VOLCANO EARS

LOVESTRUCK

PUTTING IT TOGETHER

Putting a character together starts with many rough sketches. Mix and match the simple head and body shapes you've learned so far until you get something you like. Then combine different facial features for new looks. The possibilities are endless, so don't stop with your first try.

1. Start your character by roughing in simple head and body shapes. Add some rough arms and legs.

2. Try different facial features.

3. Add details, such as hair and clothing. Try coloring in your character with crayons, markers, or paints.

PLACING HEADS

Try moving the head to different locations on the body.

way down on the chest

on top of the body

at the end of a long neck

WE'LL NEED TO USE EVERY CARTOON TRICK IN THE BOOK TO GET TO THE BARON'S IN TIME.

Smoke Trails
Add a trail of smoke behind a character to give the illusion of "burning rubber."

Speed Lines
To give the effect of speed and motion, create trailing lines behind the character.

Extreme Postures
When you run, do you run straight up and down? Probably not!

When you run, you lean forward. The farther forward your character leans, the faster it seems to be running.

Instead of leaning forward when running, your character might actually lean WAAYYY back. This gives it a panicked look.

When you blur things, it makes the character look as if it's moving very fast.

Shadows
If you add a shadow underneath your character, it looks as if it is running in the air.

25

POSING AS A MILD-MANNERED SOW SCOUT, YOU WILL TRICK VON BOREDOM INTO OPENING HIS DOOR TO PURCHASE SOME OF YOUR DELICIOUS SOW SCOUT COOKIES.

WAIT A MINUTE! A SOW SCOUT?!

THERE IS NO WAY YOU'LL GET ME IN A SOW SCOUT UNIFORM. CAN YOU PICTURE ME IN A SKIRT?

I'M NOT GONNA DO IT!

I'M NOT GONNA DO IT!

I'M NOT GONNA DO IT!

Horned Avenger Hint

Add humor to your cartoons by putting your characters in costumes and situations that might not fit their personalities. Try to think of the opposite of what the character would normally would be doing or wearing.

WHAT ARE YOU GIGGLING AT, YOU OVERGROWN BEANBAG?

27

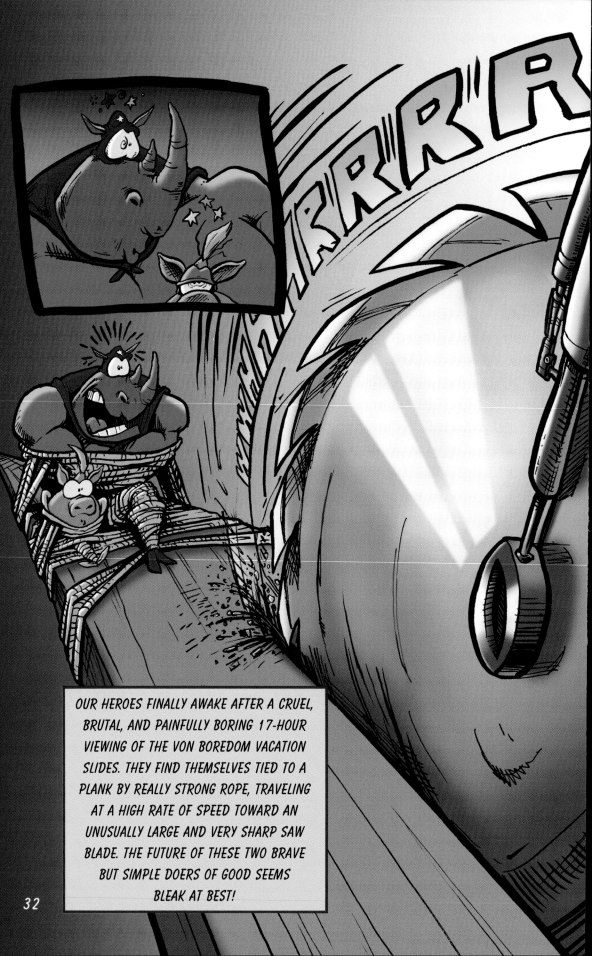

OUR HEROES FINALLY AWAKE AFTER A CRUEL, BRUTAL, AND PAINFULLY BORING 17-HOUR VIEWING OF THE VON BOREDOM VACATION SLIDES. THEY FIND THEMSELVES TIED TO A PLANK BY REALLY STRONG ROPE, TRAVELING AT A HIGH RATE OF SPEED TOWARD AN UNUSUALLY LARGE AND VERY SHARP SAW BLADE. THE FUTURE OF THESE TWO BRAVE BUT SIMPLE DOERS OF GOOD SEEMS BLEAK AT BEST!

HANDS

Speaking of grabbing, some of the most difficult things to draw are hands. Don't get discouraged! If you practice drawing hands, you will get better. At first, don't try to draw all of the joints and details of the hand. Use a circle for the palm and simple, rounded fingers.

1. Draw a circle at the end of the arm.

2. Add a thumb sticking out one side.

3. Add three or four fingers.

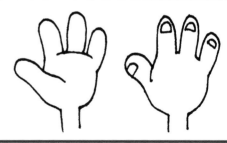

Draw long and thin fingers.

For a baby, try short and stubby hands.

When drawing the palm side, extend the thumb across the palm. If you're drawing the back of a hand, add fingernails.

MORE HANDS

HEY, H.A., DO YA THINK WE COULD LEARN ABOUT HANDS A LITTLE LATER?

GOOD POINT, PIG BOY! ERASE. ERASE LIKE THE WIND!

ERASE ERASE ERASE ERASE ERASE

LET'S ROCK AND ROLL!

BOY, AM I GLAD WE GOT OUT OF THERE!

YOU CALL THAT A SMILE, BLT?

AFTER ALL OF OUR CARTOON LESSONS, I THOUGHT YOU WOULD HAVE LEARNED THAT YOU NEED TO USE MORE EXTREME EXPRESSIONS.

YOU'RE A CARTOON! WHEN YOU'RE HAPPY, YOU'VE REALLY GOT TO SHOW IT.

Hey kids! Read Adventure #2: How to Draw Cartoon Animals to follow the continuing exploits of Horned Avenger and BLT.